GRAND CANYON
NATIONAL PARK

by J. J. Stewart

Content Consultant
Paul Hirt
Professor of History
Arizona State University

Core Library

An Imprint of Abdo Publishing
abdopublishing.com

abdopublishing.com

Published by Abdo Publishing, a division of ABDO, PO Box 398166, Minneapolis, Minnesota 55439. Copyright © 2017 by Abdo Consulting Group, Inc. International copyrights reserved in all countries. No part of this book may be reproduced in any form without written permission from the publisher. Core Library™ is a trademark and logo of Abdo Publishing.

Printed in the United States of America, North Mankato, Minnesota
082016
012017

Cover Photo: Shutterstock Images
Interior Photos: Shutterstock Images, 1; Michael Quinn/National Park Service, 4, 8, 18, 29, 34, 36, 40, 45; AP Images, 10; Kristen M. Caldon/National Park Service, 12; Dorling Kindersley/Thinkstock, 15; Grand Canyon National Park Service, 21; Red Line Editorial, 24; Tom Bean/Alamy, 26; National Park Service, 32, 42–43

Editor: Mirella Miller
Series Designer: Ryan Gale

Publisher's Cataloging-in-Publication Data

Names: Stewart, J. J., author.
Title: Grand Canyon National Park / by J. J. Stewart.
Description: Minneapolis, MN : Abdo Publishing, 2017. | Series: National parks
    | Includes bibliographical references and index.
Identifiers: LCCN 2016945461 | ISBN 9781680784732 (lib. bdg.) |
    ISBN 9781680798586 (ebook)
Subjects: LCSH: Grand Canyon National Park (Ariz.)--Juvenile literature.
Classification: DDC 917.91/32--dc23
LC record available at http://lccn.loc.gov/2016945461

CONTENTS

CHAPTER ONE

A RIVER CARVES A CANYON

At Grand Canyon National Park, there are many things to explore and experience. The Colorado River cuts through the park. It divides the park into northern and southern sections. Along the South Rim, near Bright Angel Trail, a park ranger points out a fossil in a rock to curious visitors. Elsewhere a field biologist tracks a California condor. She sweeps an antenna back and forth. Soon

The South Kaibab Trail offers beautiful panoramic views of the canyon.

Saving the California Condors

In 1982 California condors faced extinction. Twenty-two wild condors survived worldwide. Researchers blamed habitat loss and hunters. An effort was made to save the birds. Condors were captured and bred by biologists at California zoos. In 1996 six captive-bred condors were released near the Grand Canyon at Vermilion Cliffs. The condors wear radio transmitters for monitoring. Accidental lead poisoning is the biggest threat to their survival. Hunters leave gut piles with lead bullet fragments where condors feed. More than 400 condors survive worldwide today. Three mating pairs nest within the park.

her receiver picks up a signal. Nearby tourists grab their binoculars. They are excited to spot the endangered raptor in midflight.

Farther east, hikers trek down the South Kaibab Trail. They see the Colorado River below. On the river, life-jacketed rafters approach rapids. Their stomachs tense in excitement. Elsewhere in the park on the canyon's North Rim, a tourist catches her breath. She looks around in awe of the sunset-colored buttes, mesas, spires, and temples.

Discover the Grand Canyon

Grand Canyon National Park is in northwestern Arizona. The Colorado River created the canyon. The water began cutting through Earth's crust 6 million years ago. Over time the river's swift waters wore away stone. Measured by the river, the park is 277 miles (446 km) long. At its widest point, the Grand Canyon measures 18 miles (29 km) across. It is 1 mile (1.6 km) deep. The Grand Canyon is so big astronauts can see it from space.

The North Rim has fewer visitors than the South Rim because it is far from cities and interstate highways.

Each year, more than 5 million people visit Grand Canyon National Park. It is the second most visited national park in the United States. The South Rim has three visitor centers. Grand Canyon Visitor Center is near Mather Point. This is where most people see the canyon for the first time. Desert View Visitor Center is near the park's east entrance. The newest is Verkamp's Visitor Center in the historic Grand Canyon Village. For more than 100 years, the Verkamp family ran a store here. The visitor center now has exhibits about pioneer lives.

The North Rim Visitor Center is open May through October. The North Rim is 1,000 feet (305 m) higher in elevation than the South Rim. It is cooler in the summer and gets more snow in the winter. The National Park Service (NPS) closes the road to the North Rim in winter due to deep snow.

Becoming a National Park

The Grand Canyon has been home to humans since the last Ice Age approximately 13,000 years ago. Many American Indian tribes have ties to the area. Their stories tell how the Grand Canyon was formed. Beginning in the 1500s, American Indians shared their knowledge of the canyon with explorers. Many explorers wanted to profit from mining, logging, ranching, and hunting in the Grand Canyon area.

The first legislation to protect the canyon came in 1893. President Benjamin Harrison created the Grand Canyon Forest Reserve. Its goal was to manage the forest responsibly. Then President Theodore Roosevelt made an important speech at the

Early expeditions raised public awareness of the Grand Canyon.

Grand Canyon in 1903. He argued for its protection
from development. In 1908 Roosevelt made the
Grand Canyon a national monument. Finally, in 1919,
President Woodrow Wilson made the Grand Canyon
a national park. The park was later designated
a UNESCO World Heritage Site in 1979. These
sites have special protection to preserve them for
the future.

Park ranger Ann Posegate reflected on working at the Grand Canyon in a 2013 article in the *Washington Post:*

> *The first time I hiked to the bottom of Grand Canyon National Park, I knew I wanted to work there.*
>
> *Now, as a park ranger for the National Park Service, I share the science, history and beauty of this natural wonder with thousands of visitors from around the world.*
>
> *National parks are like outdoor museums. . . . One of my favorite parts of my job is showing children their first view of the Grand Canyon during school field trips. After walking on a trail through the forest, we arrive at the rim of a huge canyon about 10 miles [16 km] across and one mile [1.6 km] deep. Children are often amazed at the canyon's size and colors. Sometimes, they think it looks like a painting.*

Source: "What It's Like to Be a National Park Ranger." Washington Post. Washington Post, July 3, 2013. Web. Accessed April 22, 2016.

Back It Up

The author of this passage uses evidence to support her point. Write a paragraph describing the point the author is making. Then write down two or three pieces of evidence the author uses to make the point.

CHAPTER TWO

GEOLOGY WRITTEN IN STONE

Many rock layers can be seen at Grand Canyon National Park. The youngest rocks are found at the top of the canyon. The oldest rocks lie at the bottom. It is a great laboratory for studying Earth's history. Geologists study these rocks. Some of the oldest rocks in the area are called Vishnu Schist.

Layers of rock formed as sediment collected at the bottom of an ancient sea. As more time passed,

The Vishnu Schist rocks are approximately 1.7 billion years old.

Astronauts in the Canyon

In March 1964, five years before US astronauts successfully landed on the moon's surface, they were training at the Grand Canyon. The astronauts hiked to the bottom of the gorge. They needed to learn basic field geology techniques. With special permission from the NPS, the astronauts chipped rocks out of cliff sides. They learned how to interpret geological maps. They contrasted aerial photos with the landscape in front of them. These skills would come in handy when they visited the moon and collected moon rocks.

more sediment built up. The sea withdrew and then washed over the landscape many times. Each time, the sediment created a new layer. More than 20 layers of rock were laid down, one atop another. Many of the layers contain fossils.

Approximately 70 million years ago, moving pieces of Earth's crust collided. The event buckled the rock layers and pushed them upward thousands of feet. This formed the high, flat plateau that is the Grand Canyon.

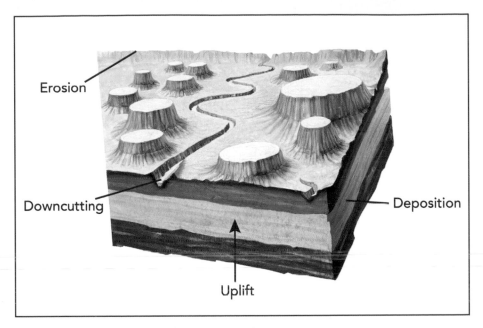

Grand Canyon Geology

Geologists have concluded the Grand Canyon was formed in four steps over many years. Deposition was the first step. Layers of sediment slowly hardened into rock. Then uplift occurred. Parts of Earth's crust collided and lifted rocks upward. Downcutting happened after. The Colorado River cut a channel in the rock. Erosion was the final step and still occurs today. Water and wind carry sediment to the bottom of the canyon, widening it. Why did layers of rock form? Can you find areas where downcutting happened in the diagram?

Approximately 6 million years ago, the Colorado River began cutting a channel downward through the plateau. The water wore away at the stone and carried it downstream. Rock layers were exposed. Smaller rivers that flowed into the Colorado River helped widen the canyon.

Trail of Time

In 2010 a University of New Mexico team, led by geologist Dr. Karl E. Karlstrom and Dr. Laura Crossey, created the Trail of Time exhibit. It is located at the South Rim. The trail helps visitors explore and appreciate geologic time. The self-guided trail begins at Yavapai Point. At first each meter marks one year into the past. Then the pace speeds up. Each meter represents 100 years, then 1,000 years, then 10,000 years, and finally, 1 million years.

Rock samples are placed at their exact geologic time points. Panels explain what was happening at that time. Visitors who complete the 2.8-mile (4.6-km) trail experience billions of years of history preserved in layers of rock.

Fossils

Many Grand Canyon fossils are shells or other pieces of marine life. The fossils are preserved in limestone, shale, and sandstone. This proves the area was once an ancient sea. Ferns, impressions of insect parts, and trilobites have been found in Grand Canyon rocks. Trilobites lived when life on Earth was beginning. Their bodies were segmented, with hinged plates. Trilobites had compound eyes with many lenses. Forty-seven types of trilobites have been identified in the park.

More advanced forms of life have also been found. Amphibian tracks have been discovered in exposed sandstone. Bones of an 11,000-year-old ground sloth were found in a cave.

CANYON DWELLERS

Grand Canyon National Park is home to many animals and plants. Within the park are different ecosystems. An ecosystem consists of all the living things in one area, along with the non-living things they depend on. Ecosystems vary in elevation, temperature, and precipitation. From Phantom Ranch at the bottom of the canyon to the North Rim's highest point, a hiker passes through five

Tall cottonwood trees provide shade near Bright Angel Creek.

ecosystems. These ecosystems are home to many different species.

Riparian Ecosystems

Riparian ecosystems are found next to year-round water sources, such as the Colorado River, waterfalls, seeps, and springs. Riparian ecosystems are not dependent upon elevation. Yellow columbine and maidenhead ferns grow out of cliff side seeps. They are called hanging gardens.

Amphibians live in or by water. In the Grand Canyon, there are four varieties of toads, two types of frogs, and two kinds of salamanders. Wildlife researchers study frogs as a bioindicator species. Frogs' disappearance or extinction signals something has harmed their environment. Northern leopard frogs were once common in the Grand Canyon. They have not been seen for several years. Wildlife researchers want to figure out why.

Desert bighorn sheep are seen on cliffs throughout the canyon.

Desert Scrub Ecosystems

Desert scrub ecosystems range from 1,200 to 4,500 feet (370–1,370 m) above sea level. Plants and animals in this type of ecosystem have adapted to hot, dry conditions. Common plants are blackbrush, sage, and prickly pear cactus. The Grand Canyon's remote location protects its bighorn sheep population. They are less likely to catch diseases spread by domestic sheep. They also cannot be hunted. The removal of feral burros in the 1970s helped the bighorns thrive. The feral burros had competed with bighorns for drinking water and plants.

Brighty of the Grand Canyon

Marguerite Henry wrote *Brighty of the Grand Canyon* in 1953. Children worldwide loved her story of a free-spirited burro named Brighty. The book was based on a real burro. The real Brighty lived at the Grand Canyon. He hauled water and gave children rides. Today children still ride into the canyon on mules. In 1928 Brighty was the first burro to cross the suspension footbridge spanning the Colorado River. A statue of Brighty sits in the North Rim's lodge.

Pinyon-Juniper Woodland Ecosystems

Pinyon-juniper woodland ecosystems exist between 4,000 and 7,300 feet (1,220–2,230 m) in elevation. They are found on or below both the North and South Rims of the canyon in sunny locations. This is the zone between desert and forest. This area receives rain and snow. Pinyon pine and Utah juniper are common here. These trees can survive for long stretches without water. Spotted skunks, javelinas, mule deer, and coyotes live here.

Ponderosa Pine Forest Ecosystems

Ponderosa pine forest ecosystems are found at both the North and South Rims. They range from 7,000 to 8,200 feet (2,130–2,500 m) in elevation. Wildflowers such as lupine grow among the ponderosa pines. A bird called the red-naped sapsucker drills holes in the tall trees. Sap seeps out. The bird eats both the sap and the bugs the sap attracts.

Kaibab squirrels are seen in this ecosystem,

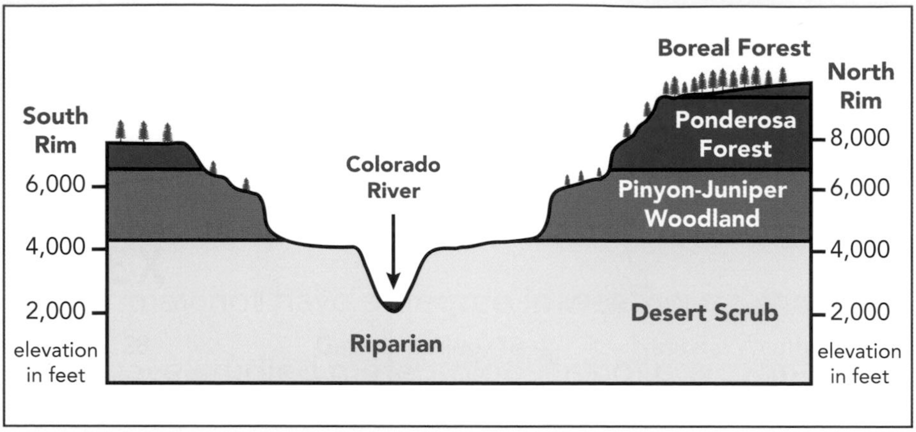
Boreal Forest
North Rim
South Rim
Ponderosa Forest
Colorado River
8,000
6,000
Pinyon-Juniper Woodland
6,000
4,000
4,000
2,000
Desert Scrub
2,000
elevation in feet
Riparian
elevation in feet

From River to North Rim

Five distinct ecosystems are found at Grand Canyon National Park. Plants and animals adapt to their environment to survive. Why do you think certain animals survive in some areas better than others? How do people adapt to the different ecosystems when they hike the Grand Canyon?

but only at the North Rim. They have black stomachs, white fluffy tails, and ear tufts.

Boreal Forest Ecosystems

Boreal forest ecosystems are found only at the North Rim. The elevation is between 8,200 and 9,200 feet (2,500–2,800 m). This area receives approximately 25 inches (64 cm) of rain a year. Up to 11 feet (3.4 m) of snow accumulates. Evergreen and aspen trees are common. Mule deer move lower when the snows begin. This is also mountain lion territory.

Important Bird Area

Scientists have observed more than 370 species of birds at Grand Canyon National Park. Some live at the canyon year round. Others stop over when they travel from place to place. The National Audubon Society has designated the park as an "important bird area." The California condor and the Southwestern willow flycatcher were listed as endangered species.

FURTHER EVIDENCE

Chapter Three focuses on the Grand Canyon's wildlife. What was one of the chapter's main points? What evidence was given to support that point? Check out the website at the link below. Choose a quote from the website that relates to this chapter. Does this quote support the author's main point? Does it make a new point? Write a few sentences about how the quote relates to this chapter.

Mammals of the Grand Canyon

mycorelibrary.com/grand-canyon

CHAPTER FOUR

PEOPLE WHO MADE CANYON HISTORY

Indigenous people have lived in the Grand Canyon area for thousands of years. Artifacts found in the park date back 12,000 years. Split twig figurines have been found in caves. Willow twigs were twisted into deer and desert bighorn sheep shapes. Archaeologists believe the figurines were ritual hunt offerings.

Split twig figurines prove that American Indians have lived in the Grand Canyon area for thousands of years.

The Tusayan Ruin and Museum in the park shows what life was like for American Indians who lived in the area. The 800-year-old ruin is an ancient Puebloan village. It is built of limestone. The roof was constructed of wooden beams. It was then covered with branches and sealed with clay. Twenty-five people lived in this village. The ancestral Puebloan Indians were the first farmers in the area. They grew corn, beans, and squash, and they hunted deer. Hopi Indians are their descendants.

Today three American Indian reservations border the park. They belong to the Navajo, Havasupai, and Hualapai people. Many tribes have strong cultural ties to the canyon.

Explorers

In 1540 Spanish soldier García López de Cárdenas led an expedition to find the Colorado River. The Hopi Indians said a great river lay to the west. Cárdenas and his men likely found the South Rim. They looked for a safe way down to the river but could not

The Grand Canyon is a sacred place for many American Indians. They share their culture with visitors.

Setting the Grand Canyon to Music

In 1916 Ferde Grofé watched the sunrise at the Grand Canyon. The experience moved him. He wanted to evoke this feeling for others by using music. In 1931 Grofé finished composing his masterpiece, Grand Canyon Suite. The orchestral piece includes five movements: Sunrise, Painted Desert, On the Trail, Sunset, and Cloudburst. Listeners hear birdsong (woodwinds), crickets (trumpets), and even mules' hooves (coconut shells).

find one. After three days, they gave up and left. An unreachable river in an impassable canyon was of no use to Cárdenas.

More than 300 years later, in 1869 and again in 1871, John Wesley Powell and a small crew rafted down the Colorado River in wooden boats. Powell was an American Civil War (1861–1865) veteran who had a passion for geology and exploring the natural world. They were dangerous journeys. Powell was the first known person to lead an expedition through the Grand Canyon. He gathered information, making recommendations for development. Powell Plateau is named for him.

Architecture

The Atchison, Topeka, and Santa Fe Railway established a route to the Grand Canyon in 1901. More people came to visit. Architect Mary Colter designed the Grand Canyon's most iconic buildings. They include Bright Angel Lodge, Hopi House, Phantom Ranch, and the Desert View Watchtower. Colter studied Puebloan Indian ruins. She chartered a plane to locate prehistoric

PERSPECTIVES
Fred Kabotie

Acclaimed Hopi artist Fred Kabotie created the Desert View Watchtower's murals. Kabotie's most famous painting depicts the snake legend. In the legend, a young man named Tiyo floats down the Colorado River in a hollowed-out cottonwood trunk. Tiyo searches for and finds the snake clan. They have the power to make rain. After many adventures, Tiyo takes their ceremonial dance back to his people.

Architect Mary Colter was famously hard to please. Kabotie remembered a disagreement with her about color matching. Kabotie said, "We didn't always agree, but I think we appreciated each other."

31

Mary Colter, right, shows off blueprint designs of a building in the mid 1930s.

towers. She wanted the Watchtower's design to be true to ancient cultures.

Colter directed her workers to use onsite rocks for construction. Her structures blended into their surroundings. Bright Angel Lodge's fireplace showcases the canyon's geology. It mimics the rock layers. By providing places to stay and shop, Colter helped make Southwest tourism popular.

In a speech made at the South Rim in 1903, President Theodore Roosevelt declared that every American should see the Grand Canyon. He argued its unique landscape should be protected for future generations:

> *In the Grand Canyon, Arizona has a natural wonder which, so far as I know, is in kind absolutely unparalleled throughout the rest of the world. I want to ask you to do one thing in connection with it in your own interest and in the interest of the country—to keep this great wonder of nature as it now is. . . . I hope that you will not have a building of any kind, not a summer cottage, a hotel, or anything else, to mar the wonderful grandeur, the sublimity, the great loneliness and beauty of the canyon. Leave it as it is. You cannot improve on it. The ages have been at work on it, and man can only mar it.*

Source: *Theodore Roosevelt.* Presidential Addresses and State Papers of Theodore Roosevelt . . . with Portrait Frontispiece. *New York: P. F. Collier & Son, 1905. Print. 370.*

Consider Your Audience

Adapt this passage for a different audience, such as your principal or friends. Write a blog post conveying the same information for a new audience. How does your post differ from the original text and why?

PROTECTING THE CANYON FOR TOMORROW

More than 5 million people visit Grand Canyon National Park annually. The NPS manages the park. It considers public safety and preservation when it makes decisions. Preserving the canyon for future visitors is important.

Park Attractions

Each visitor center has something to offer. In the main Grand Canyon Visitor Center, the 20-minute film

The Watchtower is a well-known tourist spot in Grand Canyon National Park.

At sunset on the North Rim, visitors try to capture the canyon's beauty by taking photos on the patio.

Grand Canyon: A Journey of Wonder takes viewers on a sunrise to sunset, rim to river journey through the park. The center is a good place to plan activities.

At Desert View Visitor Center, tourists can climb the Watchtower designed by Mary Colter. They view the art created by Fred Kabotie. From the top of the tower, they can see a long stretch of the Colorado River. In Verkamp's, visitors explore what it was like living and working at the Grand Canyon many years ago. The walking history timeline on the floor highlights important events in Grand Canyon history. Important national and world events are also shown. At the North Rim Visitor Center, park rangers help plan activities.

There are three ways to explore the canyon. Those who hike rim to rim sample all the Grand Canyon has to offer. They travel through five ecosystems. Backpackers visit areas unseen by those who stick to popular trails. Hikers must carry plenty of water. Temperatures at Phantom Ranch have

PERSPECTIVES
Grand Canyon after Dark

"As the sky gets darker after sunset you start to notice something on the eastern horizon that at first you think are storm clouds. Then as it gets darker you realize they aren't clouds in our atmosphere, but they are glowing clouds of stars," said astronomer John Barentine with the International Dark-Sky Association. The Grand Canyon's pristine night skies make it one of the best places to observe the Milky Way. In 2016 the Grand Canyon was provisionally designated an "International Dark Sky Park." Staff will replace certain light fixtures to attain full status by the park's 100th anniversary in 2019.

reached 120 degrees Fahrenheit (49°C). It has also snowed in June at the South Rim.

Visitors can ride mules to the bottom of the Grand Canyon. Mules have carried tourists since the late 1800s. The Colorado River offers thrills and chills for river runners. They board at Lee's Ferry and float downstream in rubber rafts.

Protecting the Canyon

It is important to protect Grand Canyon National Park. The NPS and other groups are working hard to preserve the park's natural beauty. What happens outside the park can harm or change the canyon. In the 1960s, Glen Canyon Dam began operating upriver. This has stopped large amounts of sediment from flowing down the Colorado River. It also reduced the size of sand beaches along the river. Habitat in and along the river changed forever.

Plastic water bottles were banned from being sold in the park in 2012. They once made up 20 percent of the park's trash. Now reusable water bottles are sold instead. The NPS also removes invasive species that crowd out native animals and plants. Volunteers uproot invasive plants before they produce seeds.

The Grand Canyon faces many environmental threats caused by humans. Air pollution comes from coal-fired power plants and smog drifting over from cities. Noise pollution arises from overhead aircraft and sightseeing flights. Proposed uranium mining near the canyon risks drinking water contamination. Tourist development strains precious resources. The NPS,

Grizzly Bears

In 2014 the Center for Biological Diversity (CBD) petitioned the US Fish and Wildlife Service (USFWS). The CBD wants grizzly bear habitat expanded. They also want grizzlies reintroduced into the Grand Canyon region. Around 1,500 grizzly bears now live in the United States. They are a threatened species in the lower 48 states. Expanding grizzly bear range to the Grand Canyon would help the grizzly population grow. It would also help regulate other species' populations in the area.

Visitors should be mindful of the animals and plants that live in the park.

tribal groups, environmental groups, and concerned citizens all strive to manage these threats.

Everyone can protect the Grand Canyon. Children ages four to fourteen can become junior rangers. Junior rangers explore the park. They learn about nature and history. Junior rangers inspire others to protect the environment.

All visitors can help by following a few simple rules. Stay on the trails. Do not leave any trash or other items behind. Bring home only photos and gift shop souvenirs. Leave the rocks and plants in place. Do not feed or disturb the wildlife. And finally, follow the park rangers' advice. Those who have visited Grand Canyon National Park know how special it is. It is a place for wonder. If visitors are careful and protect the land, they can travel here for years to come.

EXPLORE ONLINE

Chapter Five talks about protecting Grand Canyon National Park. The website below goes into more depth about this topic. How is the information on the website the same as the information in Chapter Five? What new information did you learn from the website?

Protecting the Park

mycorelibrary.com/grand-canyon

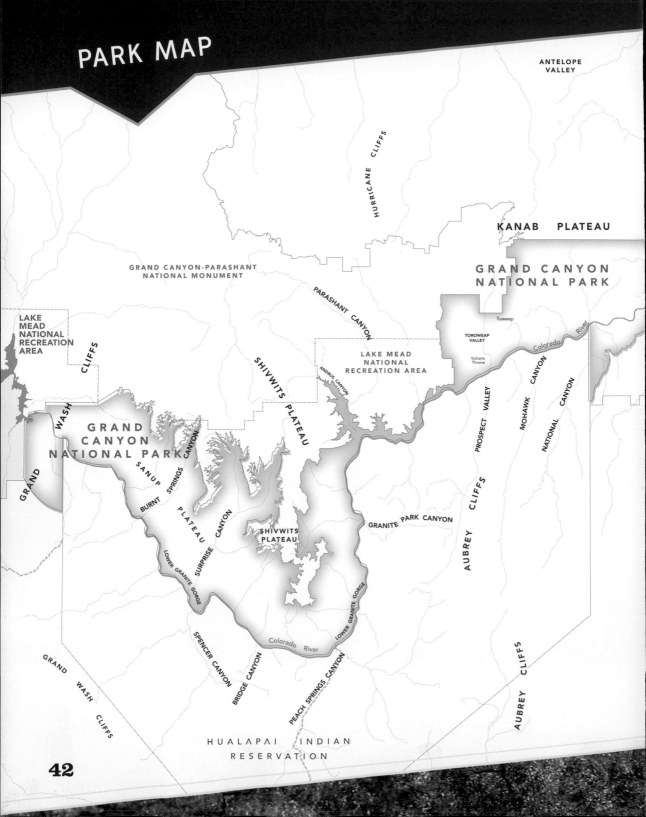

PARK MAP

ANTELOPE
VALLEY

HURRICANE CLIFFS

KANAB   PLATEAU

GRAND CANYON-PARASHANT
NATIONAL MONUMENT

GRAND CANYON
NATIONAL PARK

PARASHANT CANYON

LAKE
MEAD
NATIONAL
RECREATION
AREA

LAKE MEAD
NATIONAL
RECREATION AREA

SHIVWITS PLATEAU

ANDRUS CANYON

TOROWEAP
VALLEY

Tuweep

Colorado   River

CLIFFS

Vulcans
Throne

GRAND CANYON
NATIONAL PARK

SANUP

SPRINGS CANYON

BURNT

PLATEAU

SURPRISE CANYON

SHIVWITS
PLATEAU

GRANITE PARK CANYON

PROSPECT VALLEY

MOHAWK CANYON

NATIONAL CANYON

AUBREY   CLIFFS

GRAND

LOWER GRANITE GORGE

LOWER GRANITE GORGE

SPENCER CANYON

BRIDGE CANYON

Colorado   River

PEACH SPRINGS CANYON

GRAND WASH CLIFFS

AUBREY CLIFFS

HUALAPAI   INDIAN
RESERVATION

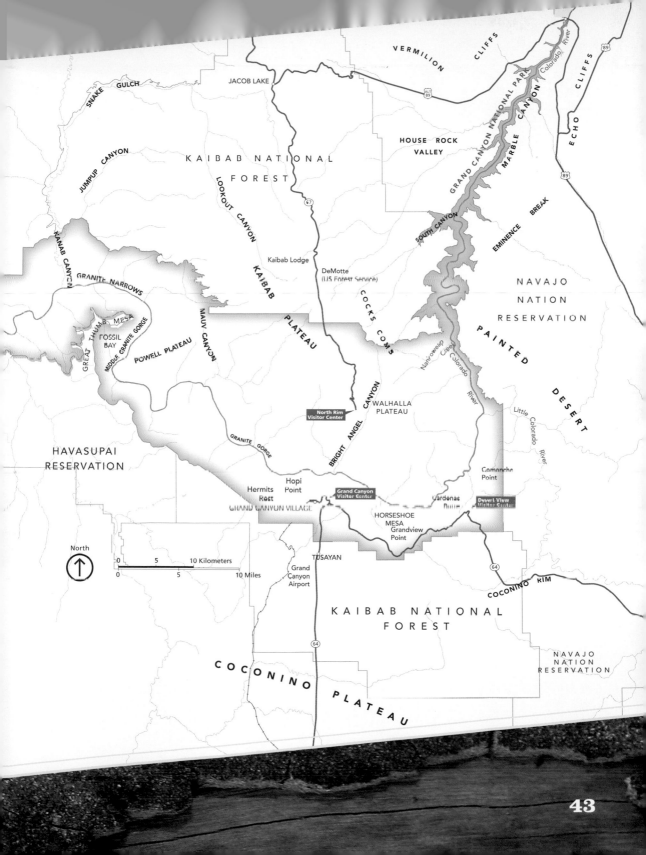

SNAKE GULCH

JACOB LAKE

VERMILION CLIFFS

JUMPUP CANYON

KAIBAB NATIONAL FOREST

LOOKOUT CANYON

HOUSE ROCK VALLEY

GRAND CANYON NATIONAL PARK

MARBLE CANYON

ECHO CLIFFS

Colorado River

89

KANAB CANYON

GRANITE NARROWS

Kaibab Lodge

DeMotte
(US Forest Service)

KAIBAB

SOUTH CANYON

EMINENCE BREAK

NAVAJO NATION RESERVATION

GREAT THUMB MESA

FOSSIL BAY

MIDDLE GRANITE GORGE

POWELL PLATEAU

MAUV CANYON

PLATEAU

COCKS COMS

PAINTED

GRANITE GORGE

BRIGHT ANGEL CANYON

North Rim Visitor Center

WALHALLA PLATEAU

Nankoweap Creek

Colorado River

Colorado River

Little Colorado River

DESERT

HAVASUPAI RESERVATION

Comanche Point

Hopi Point

Grand Canyon Visitor Center

Cardenas Butte

Desert View Visitor Center

Hermits Rest

GRAND CANYON VILLAGE

HORSESHOE MESA
Grandview Point

TUSAYAN

Grand Canyon Airport

64

COCONINO RIM

North

↑

0   5   10 Kilometers
0   5   10 Miles

KAIBAB NATIONAL FOREST

NAVAJO NATION RESERVATION

64

COCONINO PLATEAU

Tell the Tale

Chapter One of this book describes the experiences people are having at many places in Grand Canyon National Park. Imagine you are a field biologist tracking a California condor. Write 200 words about the endangered raptor. Is there anything you can do to help California condors?

Why Do I Care?

Maybe you do not live near a national park. But that does not mean you cannot think about why national parks are important. How do national parks affect your life? Do you have family or friends who have visited a national park? How do you think your life would be different if you had the chance to visit a national park?

Say What?

Studying Grand Canyon National Park can mean learning a lot of new vocabulary. Find five words in this book you have never heard before. Use a dictionary to find out what they mean. Then write the meaning in your own words, and use each word in a new sentence.

Surprise Me

Chapter Two discusses the geological history of the Grand Canyon. After reading this book, what two or three facts about the Grand Canyon's geology did you find most surprising? Write a few sentences about each fact. Why did you find each fact surprising?

GLOSSARY

archaeologist
a person who studies the bones and tools of ancient people to learn about the past

ecosystem
a community of animals and plants living together

extinction
a situation that occurs when a species dies out completely

feral
wild or undomesticated

invasive species
non-native plants and animals that damage the environment by crowding out native plants and animals

plateau
a flat area of high land

reservations
areas of land set aside by the government for a specific purpose

sediment
rock, sand, or dirt that has been carried to a place by water, wind, or a glacier

seep
a place where ground water oozes to the earth's surface

transmitter
a device that sends out radio signals

LEARN MORE

Books

Chin, Jason. *Grand Canyon.* New York: Roaring Brook, 2017.

Derzipilski, Kathleen, Amanda Hudson, and Kerry Jones Waring. *Arizona: The Grand Canyon State.* New York: Cavendish Square, 2016.

O'Connor, Jim. *Where Is the Grand Canyon?* New York: Grosset & Dunlap, 2015.

Websites

To learn more about National Parks, visit **booklinks.abdopublishing.com**. These links are routinely monitored and updated to provide the most current information available.

Visit **mycorelibrary.com** for free additional tools for teachers and students.

INDEX

ABOUT THE AUTHOR

J. J. Stewart has hiked the Grand Canyon, including rim to rim and back again, many times over the years she has lived in Arizona. She learns something new every time.